WOEFUL
SECOND WORLD
WAR

Terry Deary

Illustrated by **Martin Brown**

911 D0269040

To Stephen Shannon. With sincere thanks.

Scholastic Children's Books,
Euston House, 24 Eversholt Street,
London NW1 1DB, UK

A division of Scholastic Ltd
London ~ New York ~ Toronto ~ Sydney ~ Auckland
Mexico City ~ New Delhi ~ Hong Kong

First published in the UK by Scholastic Ltd, 1999
This abridged edition published 2013
This edition published 2018

Some of the material in this book has previously been published in *Horrible Histories: The Massive Millennium Quiz book/The Horribly Huge Quiz Book*

ISBN 978 1407 17856 1

Printed and bound in the UK by CPI Group (UK) Ltd, Croydon, CR0 4YY

2 4 6 8 10 9 7 5 3 1

Papers used by Scholastic Children's Books are made from wood grown in sustainable forests.

www.scholastic.co.uk

Contents

Introduction

History can be horrible – but some times in history are more horrible than others…

JUST LIKE LESSONS – HISTORY LESSONS ARE MORE HORRIBLE THAN GAMES LESSONS!

Of course, this is all a matter of opinion…

IF YOU ASK ME GAMES LESSONS ARE MORE HORRIBLE THAN ANYTHING IN THE WORLD!

Most people seem to agree that wartimes are the *worst* of times. And wars in the twentieth century were the *most* horrible of all. Even the winners suffered terrible losses, and new weapons weren't fussy about who they exterminated – suffering schoolkids shot, peaceful pensioners pulverized and blameless babies bombed.

You might think it's easy to drop a bomb from an aeroplane because you don't have to see the suffering you cause. But war brings out the worst side of some human beings. The monsters. The few people who enjoy the pain and torture and death they are causing...

And it brings out the best in others – the ones who risk their own lives to fight for what they think is right. The heroes and heroines.

Most people are somewhere in between. Hopefully you'll never have to suffer in a war. But you will be tested from time to time. You may like to decide if you'd act like a monster or a heroine.

Any old boring history book will tell you about the battles and the dates and the facts and figures. But what you want to know is what it was really like to live through those days. How did people really behave in the Second World War? And how would you have behaved?

What you need is a horrible history of the Second World War! So read on…

Terrible Timeline

11 November 1918

End of First World War. Germany battered and bitter. The Germans blame their leaders, traitors at home and especially the Jews. If only they can get a strong leader they will win next time…

1930s

1933

German elections won by the National Socialist party – Nat-so, or Nazi party, for short. They are led by mad, bad Adolf Hitler.

They begin bullying Jews and building up stocks of weapons. The Germans have enemies – especially Mr Stalin's Soviets – but they have friends like Mr Mussolini's Italy. Mr Churchill of Britain tries to warn the Brits but no one takes much notice … yet.

1937

In Europe two rival 'teams' are forming – the 'Allies' of Britain, France and the Soviets against the 'Axis' of Germany and Italy. The teams are spoiling for a match.

Over in Asia the Japanese attack China. So what? So their war will get mixed up with the war in Europe that is coming soon…

30 September 1938

Britain and France agree with Germany and Italy there'll be no more war. 'Peace in our time!' says Brit Prime Minister Neville Chamberlain. Fat chance.

5 October 1938

Adolf Hitler's Germans take over the Sudetenland in

Czechoslovakia … peacefully. 'I am just protecting the three million Germans who live there!' he says innocently. (Rearrange the letters of 'A. Hitler' and you get 'The Liar'!)

23 August 1939

Shock! Deadly enemies unite! Mr Adolf Hitler of Germany (with a toothbrush moustache) and Mr Josef Stalin of the Soviet Union (with a yard-brush moustache) peacefully agree not to fight one another. No chance. Never trust a man with a moustache.

1 September 1939

STALIN ONLY LIES WHEN HIS LIPS MOVE

HOW CAN YOU TELL?

A. Hitler (the liar) had promised not to invade Poland. Today his army invades Poland ... and 'peacefully' shares it with the Soviets. No one asked the Poles, of course. Britain and France say they'll fight for Poland's freedom. That means war!

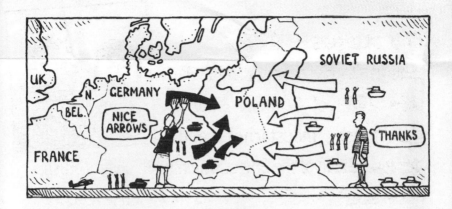

3 September 1939

Britain and France declare war on Germany. Next day Mr Winston Churchill (who doesn't have a moustache or much hair at all) is made First Lord of the Admiralty. He could say, 'I told you so!'

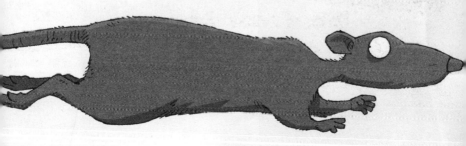

1940

9 April

Germany invades Denmark. The Danes are so surprised they don't fight back.

10 May

Brits make Winston Churchill their Prime Minister. 'I have nothing to offer but blood, toil, tears and sweat,' he says. And the blood and tears of millions of others too, of course. On the same day it's the blood and tears of the Belgians and Dutch as Germany invades.

June

Brit armies in France driven back to the beaches at Dunkirk. They escape. Mr Churchill says Brits will defend themselves in the

streets and the hills if the Germans invade. 'We will never surrender!' Tough talk for tough times. Italians (who think they know a winner when they see one) join Germany in war against the Allies.

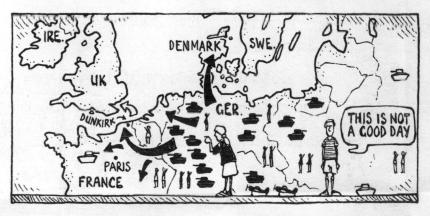

14 June

Germans enter Paris. The French say, 'We gave up without too much of a fight because we didn't want our lovely city destroyed.' Germans sneer at this feeble excuse.

7 September

German planes bomb London in daylight while British Royal Air Force hit dozens of German cities. Women and children are now in the front line of war.

December

Now Japan joins in the war on Germany's side. Italy invades Greece – just like the ancient Romans all over again – and Egypt. This is the start of war in the deserts of North Africa.

1941
10 May

Mad Hitler's madder assistant, Rudolf Hess, pinches a plane and flies to Scotland. He wants to persuade Churchill to share the world with Hitler. The Germans say Hess is potty – and many Brits agree. The Brits lock Hess up for the rest of his long life. Overnight German bombs destroy Brit House of Commons.

17

22 June

Hitler breaks his promise to Stalin (surprise, surprise), and invades Russia. Hitler makes some big mistakes but this is probably the biggest. The Soviets aren't going to give up as easily as some.

7 December

Japanese warplanes bomb the US navy in Pearl Harbor, Hawaii. US goes to war with Japan in the Pacific Ocean. Then the Japanese capture the Brit colony, Malaya. Now there's a jungle war.

HEY! THAT'S NOT FAIR, WE WEREN'T READY!

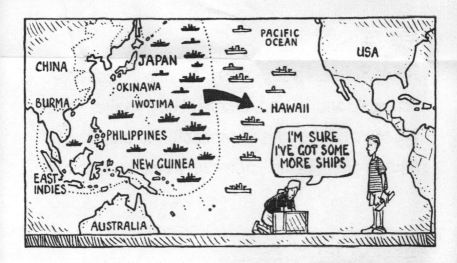

11 December

Germany and Italy declare war on the USA. This is really becoming something you can call a World War.

1942
20 January

Nastiest of all Nazi plans. German leaders meet and agree that Jews are not really human. Fit Jews will be worked to death and weak Jews will be starved or killed in death camps.

30–31 May

RAF does more damage in one night raid on Cologne than 1,300 previous attacks (it says). Meanwhile, the Soviets have pushed back the German army and the US bombed the Japanese navy. The war is turning against the Nazis.

PERSONALLY I PREFERRED THE EARLIER AIR RAIDS

7 August

In the Pacific, US marines land at Guadalcanal in the

Solomon Islands. Now the war is turning against the Japanese.

4 November

In the North African desert the British drive back the German tanks at the battle of El Alamein. That cheers up the Allies.

2 December

A nuclear reaction is created by scientists on a Chicago squash court. If this power can be turned into a bomb it could win the war. From squash court to squashed enemies. But who'll build that nuclear bomb first? The race is on.

1943
February

Germans finally defeated at Stalingrad, Russia. The Soviets start the long and bloody push towards Berlin.

19 April

Jews in Poland rise up against the Nazi exterminators. A year ago they helped the Nazis to 'evacuate' fellow Jews to the camps because they

thought it was for the Jews' own good. Now word gets back that they are, in fact, death camps. The rebels have little to lose – die fighting or die in gas chambers. But…

16 May

Jews in Warsaw wiped out. Some prefer to die in their burning buildings or jump from the roofs rather than become Nazi prisoners. Hitler's assistant, Himmler, orders the destruction of Jewish settlements everywhere.

17 May

RAF destroy German dams with a clever invention, a bomb that bounces on water. They wreck power supplies to German factories — and drown a lot of innocent people. Do not try this in your bath — either the bombing OR the drowning!

23 July

Allies are back in Europe for the first time since Dunkirk in June 1940. They capture Palermo in Sicily and head north. It's a long way – and nearly two years – from Berlin.

25 July

Italy's Benito Mussolini is thrown out of power as Italy is invaded by the Allies. Well, they have to blame someone.

1944
April

In the Pacific the US are 'island hopping' towards Japan. In Europe the Soviets

have reached Poland and Romania in the fight back to the north and east of Germany. Their Brit and US allies are heading north through Italy. All they need is an attack through France to the west and, guess what…

6 June D-Day

Allies land in France and head towards Berlin. But they're still almost a year away.

13 June

New German secret weapon, a flying bomb, lands on London. It's called the V1 – 'V' for Vergeltungswaffen … vengeance weapon. Within a month almost 3,000 Brits will be killed by them. Some weapon, some vengeance.

27

20 July

Now Hitler himself is bombed – by his own German Army officers. The bomb blows Hitler's trousers off but sadly he survives.

SO THAT'S WHAT IT FEELS LIKE

I August

The gallant Poles rebel to throw out German invaders … again. But their Soviet and American 'friends' refuse to help them. Result? Poles poleaxed.

September

First US troops set foot on German soil but the Germans fight back furiously. The end is still a long way off.

1945
27 January

Soviets march in to Auschwitz concentration camp and free 5,000 prisoners, mainly Jews. But they're three weeks too late to save the last four prisoners executed for hiding explosives. All four were young girls.

14 February

After two days of Allied air raids the ancient German city of Dresden is flattened. Statues, paintings and beautiful churches are destroyed ... and a small matter of 25,000 people. Happy Valentine's Day, Dresden.

15 February

A 15-year-old Jewish girl finished her diary three months ago with the words, 'All people are good.' Today she dies, half starved and in a fever in Belsen concentration camp. But her diary lives on as a terrible warning to us. Thank you, Anne Frank.

28 April

Italy's dictator Mussolini is tried. 'Let me live and I'll give you my empire!' he begs. Fat chance. He's shot and hanged by the heels for the people to see.

MAYBE THE SECOND WORLD WAR WASN'T SUCH A GOOD IDEA AFTER ALL

30 April

Allies surround Berlin. Adolf Hitler doesn't want to end up like Mussolini. So he kills his dog, then his new wife, Eva, and finally himself. Guards burn the body to stop it being paraded by the conquering Soviets. Many Germans refuse to believe he's dead – many more believe it and kill themselves.

7 May

New German government surrenders
and the war in Europe is over. But the most fearsome
drama of the war is still to be acted out.

6 August

US drop first nuclear bomb on the Japanese city of
Hiroshima. When a second bomb destroys Nagasaki
three days later the Japanese surrender. It's hard to
fight an enemy when a single bomb can kill
60,000 people in seconds. The Second World War
ends five years (and 40 million corpses) after it
started.

Home Horrors

The Second World War was different to past wars because you weren't safe anywhere. Innocent young people could be lying in bed reading a comic or studying at school or sitting on the toilet one moment – and be dead the next.

WE DECIDED TO PUT UP A MEMORIAL JUST WHERE IT HAPPENED

RIP JANE

Bombs could blast you, saboteurs could spifflicate you and missiles marmalize you wherever you were.

A battle area was known as a 'Front'. Now countries outside the war zones had their own 'Home Fronts'.

Horrible history happened at home as well as on battle fields...

Dad's barmy army

In Britain in 1940 the people were worried about a German invasion from the sea and from the air. The brave Brits started to arm themselves with shotguns and any weapons they could lay their hands on.

The government decided it would be better to organize these fighting folk into a proper army. In 1939 Winston Churchill had wanted a Home Guard formed – when he became Prime Minister in May 1940 he got it. Churchill had hoped for 500,000. He got 250,000 in the first day and 1,500,000 by June. They were first known as the Local Defence Volunteers – the LDV.

At first these untrained men were a bit of a joke. They weren't given proper weapons, they just armed themselves with anything that could kill. One boy said:

We were sent to defend a factory with broom handles. I pinched a knife from Mum's kitchen and tied it to the top.

One 14-year-old boy took along a bow and arrow. That would have worried some German tank commanders if the Germans really had invaded! Others took along a nice heavy golf club.

No wonder a popular comedian, George Formby, sang a song about them...

*I'm guarding the home of the
Home Guard,
I'm guarding the Home Guard's home.
All night long, steady and strong,
Doing what I told 'em,
I can't go wrong.
One evening when on LDV,
Some German soldiers I did see.* PLINK
PLINKA
PLINK
*They ran like Hell ...
but they couldn't catch me!
I'm guarding the Home Guard's home.*

The government said Home Guard soldiers had to be aged between 17 and 65. But boys as young as 14 joined. Some old soldiers from the First World War lied about their age and were 80 years old. No wonder they got the nickname 'Dad's Army'.

The men in Dad's Army were keen. It was great that they felt they were doing something to help. But sometimes they were too keen and too clumsy. Then they became Dad's disasters...

Ten horrible Home Guard facts

1 Home Guard soldiers were worried about how to spot a German. They were warned an enemy paratrooper might be disguised as a nun, a vicar or even a woman carrying a baby. The daftest idea for uncovering a spy was to shout…

HEIL HITLER!!!

…and a German couldn't stop himself from raising his arm, clicking his heels and replying…

2 Home Guards were in more danger from their own weapons than from the enemy who never arrived. They were given sticky bombs – a bit like explosive toffee apples on a stick. The idea was that they would run up to an enemy tank and slap the goo-covered bomb on to the side. But many tried to *throw* the bombs, the sticks came loose and the bombs fell at their feet. Oooops! Seven hundred and sixty-eight Home Guard members were accidentally killed during the Second World War and nearly 6,000 more were injured.

3 And their families were also at risk. A Home Guard soldier was cleaning his rifle on the kitchen table and forgot that there was a bullet in the firing chamber. He pulled the trigger, the gun went off – and killed his wife.

4 Early in the war, Home Guard soldiers seemed to believe that anyone landing by parachute must be a German. A brave RAF pilot, James Nicholson, was hit by canon fire from a German fighter. His foot was smashed and he was on fire. He stuck to his task and shot down the enemy plane before parachuting clear. As he drifted down, wounded and burning, some young Home Guards began blasting at him with shotguns. He screamed at them to stop but they were too excited to listen. Somehow he survived but was more injured by his Home Guard colleagues than by the enemy attack. (James Nicholson became the only Second World War fighter pilot to get the top medal, the Victoria Cross, for his action that day. His Home Guard attackers didn't get medals.)

5 Home Guards had to deal with reports of spies, even when those reports were a little wild. A British officer was sent to live in Winchester and was given a room in a nearby village with a vicar. The vicar's daughter immediately suspected him of being a German spy and ran to report him to the Home Guard…

You can tell that girl was keen to flush out spies! And an old woman locked a man from the electricity board in her cupboard because he had a little moustache like Hitler.

6 Schoolchildren weren't safe … not even from their school mates. Alan Chadwick enjoyed going down to the local aircraft factory after school to watch the new planes being tested. A 17-year-old Home Guard was on patrol to stop spies. As Alan cycled by the fence the guard called him to stop. Alan ignored him. The guard called again and when Alan took no notice he fired a warning shot into the ground. But the bullet bounced off the road, hit Alan in the back and killed him. Why hadn't Alan stopped when the guard called to him? Because he was deaf.

7 Some Home Guard soldiers saw themselves as a wartime police force. They set up road blocks to stop and question everyone who came that way. One man complained he was stopped 20 times on an eight-mile journey!

Even a local milkman was sent home to get his identity papers. A Scottish man on the Air Raid Protection team was driving to Leuchars air base one night when he ignored a Home Guard road block. He was shot dead.

8 A government inspector was measuring a field one day when local villagers accused him of being a German spy. An old farm worker tried to protect the inspector and was shot and killed by a panicking Home Guard member. The harmless old man was 68 years old. The inspector tried to show his identity papers but he was killed too. The soldier who shot them went to prison for 12 months. During the Second World War 50 innocent Brits died at the hands of their own Home Guard.

9 Of course it was probably worse being a member of the Home Guard in Germany. A 59-year-old farmer, Karl Weiglein, was called to serve in the Nazi home defence army towards the end of the war. As the enemy drew near, the Nazis blew up a local bridge and that annoyed the farmer. He complained to one of his neighbours, 'The people who did this are idiots and ought to be hanged.' But the Home Guard commander (the local school teacher) overheard old Karl. He arranged to have him tried and then executed. The old man was hanged from his own pear tree outside his own front door while his wife watched from the window. The body was left hanging for three days as an example to anyone else who wanted to complain.

10 The French Home Guard (The Franc-Garde or the *milice*) was set up to check on illegal food supplies. If a restaurant had more food than its ration the *milice* shared it around the poor. Sounds friendly? In fact the *milice* made themselves into an extra police force, working for the German army who were occupying France. They raided homes, spied on neighbours and betrayed freedom fighters to the enemy forces. A French survivor explained…

> *When you walk through French streets there are blue signs that say, 'Jacques Dupont was shot here by the Germans.' But they never say, 'Jacques was first betrayed by Frenchmen working for the Nazis.'*

The British 'Dad's Army' could be a danger to themselves and to the British people … but other Home Guard armies could be far more cruel.

Secret army

By 1942 the British Home Guard were given proper training and good weapons. No one knows how much use they'd have been if Britain had been invaded. But there was *another* group of fighters who would have had a good chance against invaders.

They were a secret army of highly trained commandos who were given the very best weapons and underground hide-outs. How did this special force stay secret? Was it because...

a) They only trained at night when everyone was asleep?

b) They trained on a deserted island off the coast of Scotland where there were only sheep to spy on them?

c) They pretended they were ordinary Home Guard soldiers?

Answer

c) Britain's secret army trained and dressed like Home Guard but were ruthless and tough. One day a farmer approached them and said, 'You don't fool me! I know your secret!' The soldiers decided they would have to kill him … if the Germans ever landed. 'We would have done it too,' an old soldier said.

Fighting French

In 1940 the Germans came to France and liked it so much they stayed. There were reports of German Officers shaving with champagne. The Germans stayed in the north and east of France and ran it as if it were Germany – it was known as 'Occupied' France.

They very kindly let the French run the south and west of the country from the town of Vichy – and

---

1 Actually they shaved with razors and just rinsed them in champagne, but you know what I mean.

that was known as 'Vichy' France. Of course, the French in Vichy, France had to be well-behaved and act like little Germans or they'd be punished.

The Germans didn't want people from Occupied France going backwards and forwards to Vichy France, taking out secret information and bringing in weapons. The border was closed.

Oh, and there was a third bunch of French – the 'Free' French, led by General Charles de Gaulle who had escaped to England when the Germans arrived.

The German secret police (the Gestapo) made it pretty miserable in Occupied France, so secret groups began to resist German rule – they were the 'Resistance.'

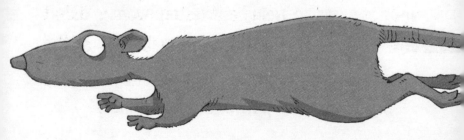

Winston Churchill and the Brits decided to help the Resistance by setting up the SOE – (Special Operations Executive) – a group so secret that no one outside even knew it existed.

By 1942 there were secret agents in France to help make life tough for the Germans. While Soviet women fought in tank battles and the trenches, Western women didn't fight in the big battles of the Second World War. But they did play a brave and vital part in the Resistance.

Terror for traitors

Germany occupied several countries and in every one they found some local people willing to help them – 'collaborators'. But not all collaborators got off lightly.

In Poland, a Resistance fighter described how he dealt with a collaborator...

A man who informed on us to the Germans lived in the village of Srednie Lany. We marked him down for execution. We went to his house at night, tied him up and made him give us the names of other Nazi informers in the surrounding villages. We also asked for the names of the people he'd betrayed. After that we called all the villagers together, read out the death sentence and carried it out on the spot. To protect the villagers against Nazi revenge I left behind a note which read: 'This is what will happen to anyone who works for the Germans.'

The Germans weren't popular in Poland. They took all the best food for themselves and the people of the occupied country went hungry. That's why they rebelled.

A Polish tax collector had the job of stapling metal tags to the ears of pigs to show they belonged to the Germans. Resistance workers entertained some villagers by grabbing the tax collector and fastening the tags through his ears. Ouch!

Women also suffered revenge attacks. A French woman fell in love with a German soldier. When the war was over the villagers came to get her...

*When they came for me I thought they
would break down the door.
I was frog-marched into the street
where men and women held me down.
Their faces were twisted with hate and
they called me a traitor. Then
somebody grabbed a handful of hair
and started hacking away with a pair
of scissors. I tried to hide my fear but I
almost choked when I saw the flash of
a razor. It was scraped across my head
painfully. The crowd were cheering and
howling. They painted swastikas on my
head using mud from the gutter. I have
never felt so wretched in my life.*

57

Of course it wasn't only in France that traitors were punished by their own people. In Russia a Resistance fighter wrote…

We shot a traitor. In the evening I went to do the same to his wife. We are sorry that she leaves three children behind. But war is war!

And murder is murder.

Fighting females

The heroes and heroines of the Resistance deserve a book of their own. These are just four examples of the work some heroines did and the things they suffered.

Name: Yvonne Cormeau

Code name: Annette

History: When her husband was killed in the London Blitz she joined SOE as a radio operator and parachuted into France. She was almost caught when agent 'Rodolph' betrayed her group. She received a bullet wound in the leg while fighting with the Resistance. She travelled through France disguised as a district nurse. When stopped at a German checkpoint her radio equipment was examined. She told the German guards it was her X-ray machine – and they believed her!

End: Survived the war. Died in January 1997, aged 88. Her blood-stained briefcase and dress with a bullet hole can be seen in the Imperial War Museum, London.

Name: Dianne Rowden

Code name: Paulette

History: An English girl who had lived with her parents in the south of France and loved the country. When the Nazis invaded she decided to try and help the French gain their freedom. She was landed in France in 1943 but didn't know that traitors had already betrayed her Resistance group. She was followed from the moment she landed, so every time she visited a contact she was accidentally betraying them! After a month the Gestapo arrested her and tortured her. She refused to talk.

End: In May 1944 the Allies were ready to invade Europe. The Nazis worried that Dianne could be freed and would tell the British who the traitors were. So she was taken to a prison camp in Germany. A doctor told her he was giving her an injection to protect her against typhus. In fact, he was injecting her with poison. Her body was 'evidence' so it was destroyed in an oven.

Name: Violette Szabo

Code name: Louise

History: Violette's husband was killed fighting with the Free French forces in North Africa. She decided to join the Resistance to avenge him. But Violette didn't want to be a radio operator – she said she wanted to 'fight with a gun in my hand.' After running into a German patrol in June 1944 her group fled but Violette twisted a weak ankle, injured in parachute practice. She held off the Germans while her companions escaped and was finally captured.

End: Violette was sent to Ravensbruck Concentration camp. She believed that being British would protect her, but in February 1945 she was taken from her cell and shot in the back of the neck. A book and a film called *Carve Her Name With Pride* were written to tell her story.

Name: Odette Sansom

Code name: Celine

History: Travelled through Vichy, France carrying messages and codes for her group leader, Peter Churchill. When they were caught she tried a daring lie, saying she was married to Peter and they were related to British Prime Minister Winston Churchill. She was tortured to betray her secrets. First her toe nails were torn out one by one but she refused to talk. Then she was locked in an empty underground cell with no light and only a board to sleep on. As a child she'd been blind, so the weeks of darkness didn't frighten her either.

End: When the Germans were defeated Odette's lie about Churchill paid off. As the Allies approached the concentration camps many secret agents were executed to silence them for ever. But not Odette. The commander of her camp decided to take her to the Allied forces personally and say, 'Here is a relation of your Winston Churchill. I saved her. Take care of me.' She survived and became famous for her courage with a book and a film (both called *Odette*) about her war deeds.

Resistance dangers

Living in another country means more than simply learning to speak the language. There are dozens of ways you can give yourself away…

Oooops! 1

A woman SOE agent was parachuted into France from England. She arrived safely in a large town. But when she came to cross the road she looked carefully to her right … and was almost knocked down by a truck that was coming from her left. She simply forgot that the foolish French have the crazy habit of driving on the wrong side of the road!

The good news is the truck missed her. The bad news is that a Gestapo officer saw what she did, guessed her secret, and arrested her.

Oooops! 2

'Annette' was dropped into the Gascogne region of France. It was the custom of women there to wear jewellery in public. 'Annette' arrived with no jewellery so she stood out. She also had to learn that the locals didn't sip soup from the side of the spoon and women didn't walk with such long strides as hers.

The clumsiest mistake was to give her a cover story that said she was from Occupied France in the north and had moved to Vichy France in the south. To do that she'd have to cross the border and have her papers stamped. The stamp was missing from her false papers. Somehow 'Annette' survived the careless way she was prepared.

Oooops! 3

Secret agents were given large amounts of money to carry into France. The money was to buy weapons and other equipment and make sure the resistance groups could buy food.

Freedom fighters in the Balkans area of Europe knew that British agents would land with a money belt stuffed with cash. So some of the agents were murdered as soon as they landed. The fighters said, 'Thanks for the money, we don't need you!'

One British agent, Nigel Low, had a criminal record for stealing money from his company before the war. He was trained as an agent, given a large amount of cash and dropped in France. He simply ran off with it and was never seen again. A case of...

THANKS FOR THE MONEY. I DON'T NEED YOU!

Polish pain

When the Nazis invaded Poland in 1939 their friends (for the moment) the Soviets marched in from the east and took areas of Poland that used to belong to them 20 years before.

The Soviets didn't want the Polish Army to fight back, so in April and May 1940 they...

• took all the Polish officers to the forest of Katyn where there was a large pit dug amongst the trees
• shot the Polish officers in the back of the head
• threw them into the pit and buried them ten layers deep.

The Soviets then tried to cover the graves with freshly planted trees and the tracks leading to the grave were grassed over. Still, three years later, the German army discovered the mass grave.

Who did the Soviets blame? They blamed the Nazis who'd passed that way when they invaded Russia!

 IT WASN'T ME GUV, HONEST!

Stamping out trouble

The Soviets also imprisoned enemies inside Poland. Anyone who had connections around the world was an enemy. So all of the area's stamp collectors were rounded up and … stamped out.

When they later invaded Latvia their records show they shot a woman because…

She was caught singing a Latvian folk song

...while some Germans shot any Russian peasants who could read and write. 'Anyone who is clever enough to read and write,' they said, 'is clever enough to cause trouble.'

The Soviet prison officers in Latvia were utterly brutal. Every prisoner who came to them was tortured. But they weren't the carefully planned tortures that the Nazis used. The Soviet jailers...

• beat prisoners with railings broken from fences

• crushed their fingers in the doors of their cells

• put thin books over their heads and beat them with hammers (because they wanted to cause pain, not death from a fractured skull).

One poor prisoner had his private parts wrapped in paper that was then set alight.

Whole families of Poles, Latvians, Lithuanians and Estonians were sent to Soviet prison camps in Siberia. The conditions in the trains taking them were so bad that when they stopped at stations the dead would be thrown out on to the platform.

When they arrived in Siberia things were worse. In temperatures of minus 40 degrees they had to live in holes in the ground or huts made of straw and branches. The men, women and children who survived the cold were worked to death.

When their German 'friends' invaded Russia in the summer of 1941, the Soviet jailers wiped out their prisoners in Poland with unbelievable cruelty. Sticks of dynamite were thrown in to one cell full of women prisoners. Another cell floor was found scattered with the eyes, ears and tongues of the dead prisoners.

The Soviets were as savage as their new enemies, the Nazis.

Winners and losers

For the first year of the Second World War the people outside the battle zones were hardly affected by the war. But the longer it went on the more difficult, dangerous and deadly it became, whether you were in Munich, Manchester, Milan or Moscow.

There were winners, and there were losers, as there are in times of peace.

Winners at war...

1 Coca Cola

Coke had a 'good' war. It was supplied at a nickel a bottle to US soldiers. Coca Cola controlled 95 per cent of the overseas soft drinks market. During the war, US soldiers drank ten billion bottles. In 1939, Coca Cola had only five overseas bottling plants. By 1945, they had 64. What made it so popular?

Because the water was so disgusting. The army kept it clean by adding chlorine – so it tasted like your local swimming pool. Sometimes water was carried in old petrol tanks or oil drums just to add to the flavour. Their powdered coffee was dreadful, fruit juice was known as 'battery acid' and 'lemonade crystals' made a drink that tasted of disinfectant. Alcohol was banned in the US forces – one tank crew got their hands on an enemy supply of champagne and almost ran over a jeep – a jeep carrying their general.

2 Cigarette makers

If you want to get on in the war then own a cinema. People who went to the cinema smoked heavily in the 1940s. One owner went around and collected the cigarette ends from the floor, took out the tobacco and turned them into new cigarettes. They were named 'RAF' – perhaps because they were 'Really Awful Fags'. The manufacturer was sent to prison for his illegal manufacture of these killer weeds but his cigarettes still kept turning up at the Front ... so someone was still 'winning' during the war.

3 Black marketeers

When food was scarce it often replaced money. It was against the law to trade food without ration books. People who did were known as racketeers and when they were caught in Germany they could be shot.

Three Nazi Ministers were suspected of being racketeers in 1944. They were investigated but their case was handled by Berlin's Chief of Police … one of their racketeer friends! So, were they arrested, tried and punished? Don't be daft! Of course they weren't!

A Berlin waiter ran a 'Black Market' business – he could get things for people when they were in really short supply on ration – petrol, perfume, food and drink. This man made so much money he was able to retire to a big house with an estate in the country. He was rich but had taken great risks. Even people caught hunting through bombed ruins to take valuables were dealt with savagely.

4 The German chemical industry

At the start of the war a German chemical company known as I G Farben was the largest in the world. But its huge success was based on cheating. While everyone else in the world had to pay their workers, I G Farben used slave labour. The concentration camps were packed with rounded-up prisoners and I G Farben was able to pay the Nazis five Reichmarks a day for each prisoner they used – the prisoner, of course, got nothing but hard work and was basically a slave. The people who ran the factories argued with the people who ran the concentration camps...

IT'S YOUR JOB TO FEED THE SLAVES!

Of course the result was neither fed the prisoners properly and they died quickly.

When the exhausted prisoners dropped down dead they were replaced with new prisoners. The Nazis built a forced labour camp at Auschwitz to provide slave labour for I G Farben's artificial rubber plant. The prisoners were fed thin turnip soup and bread that was full of sawdust. On average, they only survived for three months.

But some prisoners' fate was even worse than slavery and starvation. Scientists and doctors were allowed to use prisoners for gruesome experiments with new drugs and chemicals and surgery. At Auschwitz, Doctor Josef Mengele was obsessed by twins, and once sewed two gypsy children together to try and create Siamese twins.

In 1942 two prisoners did escape from Auschwitz and reported the death camps to the Allies. 'Please flatten them with your bombers,' they begged. But the Allies decided it would risk too many of their pilots and crew. The deaths went on.

...and war's losers

1 Vienna postmen

Families in Austria tried to cheer up their fighting men by sending them chocolate and soap. But the army couldn't always deliver these so they sent them through the post. Chocolate and soap were scarce and valuable so a group of 17 postmen began opening the parcels, stealing the contents and selling them. The law enforcers of Vienna were not amused. The postmen were taken to the main square in Vienna and shot in public so everyone could see what happened to such despicable thieves. That's life – Postman Pat one minute, postman splat the next.

2 A Berlin family

One Berlin family were definitely war losers ... they lost their grandfather! Here's how it happened...

So let that be a lesson. Wrapping wrinklies in wrugs is wrong!

3 German radio fans

It was against the law to listen to foreign radio broadcasts in wartime Germany. Anyone caught would be punished.

What a silly law! How would the police know what you listen to in your own living room?

Er ... actually there were little spies in German homes. Young people in the Hitler Youth organization were told they must report their parents if they listened to enemy radio.

YOU'D BETTER GIVE ME MORE ICE CREAM, OR ELSE!

Many Hitler Youth members did just that. An Austrian ballet dancer went to prison for three years after his daughter split on him.

Would you betray your poor parents? On second thoughts … better not answer that!

It wasn't just children who betrayed family. One woman told the Gestapo to listen under her window while her husband criticized Hitler – the poor man got four years in jail. It's cheaper than a divorce.

But how's this for gratitude…

But it was a dangerous game, informing on others. A railway worker lied about a woman neighbour and he was proved to be lying. He was shot.

4 The people of Leningrad

In the winter of 1941–42 the Germans surrounded the Soviet city of Leningrad. Hitler decided not to waste German soldiers by entering a mined and booby-trapped city. He would use the ancient tactic of 'siege'. So the Germans surrounded the city, bombed it every day, and waited for the Soviets inside to starve and freeze to death. Many did.

In January 1942 a Leningrad doctor visited a family. He described what he saw…

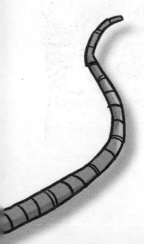

A horrible sight met my eyes. It was a dark room, covered with frost and puddles of water on the floor. Laid out on some chairs was the corpse of a 14-year-old boy. In a pram was the body of a tiny baby. On the bed lay the owner of the room, dead. At her side stood her eldest daughter, rubbing her with a towel to try and revive her. In one day she had lost her baby, her brother and her mother, all perished with the hunger and the cold.

It's horribly true, but not surprising, that some of the starving people of Leningrad removed the arms and legs of the corpses and ate them. Cannibalism was the only way that some survived.

Yet the savage winter hurt the German attackers too. In time they were driven back and defeated. The starving of Leningrad may have been winners after all.

Firestorm fury

In a war you have to believe that you are fighting for the right side. When the Second World War started on 3 September 1939 the British Prime Minister, Neville Chamberlain, told his people:

It is evil things that we shall be fighting against – brute force, bad faith, injustice, oppression and persecution.

In the USA in 1942 a poster showed the boxing champion Joe Louis with a rifle and neatly buttoned uniform saying:

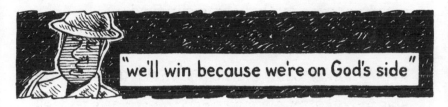

"we'll win because we're on God's side"

The truth is that the other side believe exactly the same thing – and God doesn't usually take sides.

War is horrible but the Second World War was especially horrible because so many millions of *innocent* civilians were killed, bombed in their home towns, miles behind the battle front. Here are just ten gruesome facts about a bombing raid when the enemy destroyed a city without mercy.

Only one fact is wrong. Which one?

London – 13 February 1945

1 It was Shrove Tuesday and a carnival day. A day for children to forget the war, dress up in bright costumes and have a parade through the city streets. The circus was performing to a thousand happy families and there was no warning of what was to come.

2 First came the pathfinder planes. They found the city and dropped red marker bombs that hovered 200 metres above the city centre and marked the way for the bombers. Home Defence fighters took off to shoot them down but the panicking gunners on the ground shot down their own planes. People who saw the flares ran for cover and the shelter of the cellars. But no air-raid siren sounded.

3 The last act of the circus began and clowns rode donkeys into the ring. That's when the warnings finally rang out.

> *The first waves of a large enemy bomber formation have changed course and are now approaching the city boundaries. There is going to be an attack. The population is instructed to proceed at once to the basements and cellars. The police have instructions to arrest all those who remain in the open.*

4 At 10:13 p.m. the first bombs fell. They were shattering high explosives that brought down buildings and trapped citizens in their shelters below the ground. But the worst was still to come. The fires, greedy for oxygen, sucked in air and winds rushed to feed them. The fires grew hotter, sucked harder, and the winds grew stronger and stronger and stronger. This was the fire storm effect the bombers wanted. It was a whirlwind of flames that uprooted trees and sucked people off their feet into the heart of the fire.

5 The next wave of bombers arrived at 1:30 a.m. They were carrying fire bombs that spread a blazing liquid over the city and turned it into a massive bonfire. They had no trouble finding the city. They could see the fires from the first wave from 200 miles away. This time the home fighter planes stayed on the ground. No one knows why – some think the links to their aerodrome were cut. The bombers had the freedom of the skies to drop their deadly fire bombs wherever they wanted. Of the 1,400 enemy aircraft that flew over the city that night only six failed to return. As the circus tent collapsed in flames the dappled grey Arab horses huddled in a frightened circle. Their glittering costumes were seen shimmering in the light of the fires.

6 Wednesday dawned. Ash Wednesday. Survivors crawled out of the rubble that was once a city centre. A three-mile cloud of yellow-brown smoke drifted over the city and carried charred debris that fell on a prisoner-of-war camp 15 miles away. Ash Wednesday. Then the third flight of bombers arrived to rain down a further 11 minutes of death. Long-range enemy fighters flew low and machine-gunned anything or anyone that moved. One plane machine-gunned a children's choir.

7 Some of the people in the cellars had weakened the walls that joined their house to the ones next door. When their escape to the street was blocked they broke down the walls into other houses again and again, looking for a way out. But smoke from the fires rolled down and choked them. An army officer, home on leave, saw 60 people in a cellar, their escape barred by a fire. He tried to help them...

The ones who refused to take his advice died.

8 One of the main targets had been the station. That morning children's bodies were stacked there in a huge mound. Many were still wearing their bright carnival costumes. But the station wasn't destroyed. By the next day the trains were running again. So tens of thousands of people had died and the enemy had gained very little.

9 Then the job of counting the cost began. For a week after the raid the city was filled with unburied dead. Bodies were lined up on the pavement to be

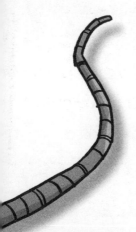

identified. Rescue workers were given cigarettes and brandy to mask the smell. Prisoners of war were brought in to help with the work – but the citizens attacked them. They had to take their revenge on someone.

10 Bodies were buried in mass graves but there were no coffins and no sheets. Many were simply wrapped in newspapers, some in empty paper cement bags. There were too many dead to count. Some guesses say that it was 25,000.

Answer

Terrible but true. The only 'wrong' fact is the first word of the title. For this *wasn't* London destroyed by Nazi monsters. This was Dresden in Germany, bombed by the RAF by night and the US Air Force by day – with God on their side, of course.

Frightful Fighting

Most of the fighters in the Second World War hadn't chosen to be soldiers ... they were normal people like your parents and teachers. (Well some teachers are fairly normal.) They joined the fighting forces and could be ordered to do some things they'd never have dreamed of doing in everyday life. Not just killing strangers – but killing them in some pretty nasty ways...

Shooting strangers

Sometimes you may be ordered to do something horrific in times of war. The trouble is you may have to spend the rest of your life with the terrible act on your conscience. Here is a true case. Imagine it happened to you.

• You are a British soldier in Burma, marching through the jungle towards the Japanese enemy.

• Your patrol captures three Burmese villagers and a ten-year-old boy who are almost certainly spying for the Japanese.

• If you let them go they will report your position to the enemy and the lives of all of your comrades will be in danger.

• The officer decides the Burmese must be shot and he selects you to be one of the firing squad.

What do you do?

a) Refuse and ask if someone else can do the shooting.

b) Agree to shoot the men but plead to let the boy live.

c) Obey. Shoot the three men and the boy.

The choice

You have *no* choice in fact.

If you **a)** refuse, then the officer could have you shot, and the four spies will die anyway.

The soldier in the actual story tried **b)**, and begged the officer to let the boy live. The officer explained that if the boy escaped he would betray them all and everyone could die. The boy would have to be guarded 24 hours a day and that would be difficult.

The soldier was forced to obey **c)**, even though the nightmare of the shooting lived with him 50 years after the event. He explained:

> *The boy faced us without a blindfold. As he was the second to be executed it meant he'd already seen his friend shot. When it came to his turn he was in a dreadful state. From close range the rifle fire made a terrible mess. It's something I've never been able to forget.*

That's war. It affects the survivors as well as the victims. Many soldiers left the war with terrible memories like this.

Quick quiz

Fighting isn't the clean and tidy adventure it looks in many war films. Fighting can be disgusting. How disgusting? Can you guess the answers to these questions?

1 The British army sailed to Italy but many were sea sick. Where did they throw up?

a) Over the side of the ship.

b) Into wet paper bags that burst.

c) They shared a big oil drum that steadily filled up.

WELL...THE BIG DRUM WAS FULL BUT THE GOOD NEWS IS THAT IT'S FALLEN OVER SO NOW IT'S EMPTY AGAIN

2 On Guam Island in the Pacific there were some unusual 'winners' in the battle between the Japanese defenders and the US attackers. What were they?

a) Frogs.

b) Flies.

c) Sharks.

DID YOU HEAR ABOUT THE DYING FROG?

IT CROAKED!

SO MUCH FOR SHARK HUMOUR

3 The British fought the Japanese at Kohima in India and sheltered in trenches. What did they use as shields?

a) Dead Japanese soldiers.

b) Dead horses.

c) Boxes of Bibles.

4 American paratroopers were safer than British because…

a) They had springs in the heels of their boots to make landings softer.

b) They had two parachutes.

c) They were fatter and the fat protected them from being hurt when they landed.

5 The Germans chose non-smokers to go on patrol against the Soviets in 1941. Why?

a) Because non-smokers have a better sense of smell and they could sniff out the enemy.

b) Because smokers gave away their position with lit matches and clouds of smoke.

c) Because smoke got in the eyes of the smokers and stopped them shooting straight.

THOSE CRAFTY SOVIETS ARE USING A SMOKE SCREEN

6 German soldiers needed good boots for the Russian winter. After killing 73 Soviet soldiers their commander ordered them to take their boots. But the boots were frozen to the feet of the Soviets. What did the commander order?

a) 'Leave them.'

b) 'Soak them in petrol, set fire to them and thaw them out.'

c) 'Saw the legs off.'

AND PUT THE FIRE OUT!

7 The Italian commander in North Africa died before he could take charge of his forces. How?

a) He fell off a camel and broke his neck.

b) His plane was shot down by his own army.

c) He was bitten on the behind by a scorpion that was sleeping on his chair.

8 Why did a Nazi torturer in Paris work dressed only in his underpants?

a) Because the water torture would spoil his clothes.

b) Because the red-hot pokers had set fire to his trousers.

c) Because the Gestapo dragged him out of bed to question a suspect and he hadn't time to get dressed.

Answers

1c) The soldiers were kept below the decks so they couldn't throw up over the side of the ship the way your dad did on the ferry to France. During the day they had the hatches above them open, but at night the hatches were closed and the air was suffocating. That's when many men were sick. They shared a large oil drum. As the ship rolled over the waves, the vomit sloshed around in the drum. Slop – slurp – slosh! (Hope you're not reading this just after your delicious school dinner?) When Allied troops sailed across the

English Channel to invade France the American soldiers were given seasickness pills – the Brit soldiers were given paper bags. One commando said:

> *The landings were a success because the men would rather face the German bullets than face going back in those boats to be seasick again.*

2b) There were too many rotting Japanese corpses for the defenders to bury. The flies had a feast. On Guam there were thousands of frogs who usually fed on the flies ... but the frogs couldn't cope! The flies simply swarmed all over the island. The US troops landed and used a strong fly repellent. It certainly kept the flies away, but the smell was so strong it led the Japanese straight to the American positions in the darkness. You had a choice – be eaten by flies or shot by the enemy.

3a) An officer wrote:

> *The place stank. The ground everywhere was ploughed up with the shell fire and human remains lay rotting as the battle raged over them. Men vomited as they dug in. In some of the trenches, rotting bodies of Japanese were used to form the parapet shield. It was almost impossible to dig anywhere without uncovering a grave or a toilet.*

4b) American soldiers jumped from their planes knowing that if their main parachute failed to open they had a spare. The Brits knew that if their parachute failed to open they would be scraped off the ground like strawberry jam. A popular paratroopers song made a joke of a parachute failure. To the tune of 'John Brown's Body' they sang:

He hit the ground, the sound was 'splat',
the blood went spurting high,
His pals were heard to say, 'Oh what a
pretty way to die.'
They rolled him in his parachute and
poured him from his boot,
And he ain't going to jump
no more!

The British Army said a second parachute would take up too much room. The truth was a second silk parachute would cost another £20 and the Army couldn't afford it. So the price of a British paratrooper's safety was less than £20.

5a) The Soviet peasant soldiers were good at hiding on the snow-covered plains – but they smelled awful. A sharp-nosed German could smell a bunch of Soviet soldiers before he saw them and had a better chance of killing them. The Soviets smelled of cheap tobacco and sweat. They also smelled of perfume that they used to kill lice in their tunics. That putrid perfume killed the lice but – if a German smelled it – it could also kill the Soviet soldier. By the way, Hitler hated tobacco and his Nazi scientists proved smoking causes cancer over 20 years before anyone else thought about it. If this Nazi science had been shared with the world then they could have saved millions of lives – which would have made a real change!

6c) Italian soldiers fighting alongside the Germans in the Russian winter had cardboard boots. The German boots weren't much better and they took Soviet army boots whenever they could get them. When they found boots frozen to dead Soviet legs their officer ordered them to saw the legs off below the knees. They carried the legs back to camp, put them in ovens for ten minutes and were able to remove the boots.

7b) Marshal Balbo flew from Italy to Libya but Italian anti-aircraft guns accidentally shot his plane down and killed him. The Italians didn't have a very happy time in the North African desert war. In September 1940 they set off in their tanks to attack the British. Unfortunately they lost their way, and drove round in a huge circle until they ran out of water and petrol. When they finally came face-to-face with the British army many Italian soldiers panicked and ran away. They were driven back into battle by their leader, General 'Electric Beard' Bergonzoli (honest, that's what they called him!). By early December they had been defeated. The Brits were surprised to find that the Italians were ready to be taken prisoner and many of them had their suitcases neatly packed and waiting to be marched off to prison. Electric Beard was shocked.

I TELL YOU WHAT JOCK, THERE'S SOME VERY STRANGE FACIAL HAIR IN THIS WAR

8a) The French Resistance radio operator, Didi Nearne, was arrested in 1944 and taken to be questioned by the Nazis. When she refused to give them the information they wanted she was sent to be tortured. The torture involved putting her in a bath of cold water and holding her head under till she began to drown. Then she was dragged upright and questioned. The torturer was stripped so he didn't get wet – but he kept his underpants on because he was embarrassed by what Didi would see if he took them off. Despite the torture she didn't betray her group. Her nasty Nazi torturer asked, 'Did you enjoy your bath?' She had the courage to smile and reply cheekily, 'Excellent!' She survived.

Funny food

One way to win a war is to starve the enemy to defeat. Cut off their food supplies. Of course, the enemy is trying to do the same to you and your people at the same time.

Britain had to bring a lot of her food from across the seas so the German submarines set out to sink the food ships. The Brits suffered. The German people suffered even worse hardships than the British.

So, if you can't eat what you want, eat whatever you can get. The US Army gave its soldiers a book with this advice…

The Bluejackets' Handbook   Page 21

Survival

When you're far from base and your rations are low then you can stay alive by turning to Mother Nature.

Remember!

• All animals are good to eat.

• Be careful about eating poisonous snakes.

• Maggots make good food.

• Grasshoppers are tasty but pull the legs and wings off before eating them.

• Do not eat caterpillars.

Isn't history amazing? That last piece of advice is 60 years old but it's still useful today. Next time you're in a cabbage patch and feeling peckish remember *not to eat the caterpillars* – with a little digging you could find a few juicy worms.

QUICK! PRETEND YOU'RE A CATERPILLAR!

US soldiers starving in Bataan found a rare food you don't get in burger bars. An officer said...

I came back from the front line and ran across three guys with a pot on the stove. I lifted the pot lid and saw a little bleached hand exactly like a baby's. It was a monkey.

MONKEY SEE MONKEY STEW

Would you have eaten a cute little monkey? You probably would if you'd been on the Bataan Hunger March. That was a forced march of 70,000 American and Filipino prisoners of war captured by the Japanese in the Philippines. Starting out on 9 April 1942, they were force-marched over 60 miles through the jungle. They were starved and often kicked or beaten on their way; many who fell were bayoneted. Only 54,000 reached the camp; 7,000–10,000 died on the way and the rest escaped to the jungle – where they ate monkeys or starved.

The Japanese officer who organized the march was executed after the war for his cruelty.

So how do you get a real feel for the war? A US soldier at Guadalcanal in the Pacific fought in the trenches in torrential rain and suggested we should all try the following game:

Dig a hole in your back garden while it is raining. Sit in the hole while the water climbs up round your ankles. Pour cold mud down your shirt collar. Sit there for 48 hours and, so there is no danger of your dozing off, imagine that a guy is sneaking around waiting for a chance to club you on the head or set fire to your house.

Get out of the hole, fill a suitcase full of rocks, pick it up, put a shotgun in your other hand and walk on the muddiest road you can find. Fall flat on your face every few minutes. Snoop round until you find a bull. Try to sneak around him. When he sees you run like hell all the way back to your hole in the back garden. If you repeat this every three days for several months you may begin to understand.

I-spy

Spies have been around for thousands of years but they become really useful in wartime. In the Third World War (due to start in the year 2033 when Martians invade) you may like to be prepared with one or two Second World War tricks.

Spy catchers were always looking for secret messages being passed to the enemy. The Germans had a hugely complex machine made to make unbreakable codes – but the Brits got a copy of the machine and cracked thousands of top-secret messages.

You don't always need clever machines for complicated codes. Two people beat the spy catchers with simple ideas. Next time you need to send that secret message to a friend try one of these genuine Second World War systems...

Comma code

Flight Sergeant Graham Hall was a terrible writer. He never used punctuation in his writing. He once joked to his wife, Vera, 'If I am ever taken prisoner and I send a letter with punctuation, then you should underline the next word. It will be a coded message.'

In June 1940 his bomber was shot down and the crew were taken to one of the famous Stalag Luft Prisoner of War (POW) camps for airmen, in north-eastern Germany. Sergeant Hall wondered if his wife remembered their joke and he tried it. It worked so well that the British secret service used him to send and receive messages from the camp – news about German weapons and troop movements, requests for help with escapes and for equipment.

You can try it. Here's an example of how it might have worked…

Dear Vera

I am alive and well. Escape from plane was dangerous. Planned to celebrate my birthday, night after we crashed. 22nd birthday if you remember. September in the garden is lovely and I'll miss it. Send my love to sis, ma, pa, N.D Jones and my other friends at the pub, local. Money I owe them will have to wait.

Love
Graham

Someone as clever as you does not need to have the message worked out, do you? [2]

The prisoners of war were allowed to receive parcels and letters from home through the Red Cross organization. They also received games like Monopoly and chess to pass the time. What the Germans didn't know was the games were specially altered to send in secret supplies – silk maps in the monopoly board, radio valves in chess pieces and hacksaw blades hidden inside a pencil. A pack of cards was actually a map in 52 pieces.

2 But for the dumb or the lazy reader, the message says, 'Escape planned night 22nd September send map and local money.' An escaper would need 'local money' once they were outside the camp and a map to find their way to the coast.

Lemon aid

One of the great secrets of the war was the Nazi concentration camps. Even German people believed that Jews were just being sent to work for the Nazi war effort. The real horror was hidden from them. Letters from the camp were destroyed if they hinted at the dreadful conditions.

But some clever prisoners managed to smuggle out the truth using the old spy trick, invisible ink.

Try it yourself. Write a postcard with a simple message, then add the real message in invisible ink.

Lemon Spy!

YOU NEED THE JUICE OF A LEMON, A THIN PAINTBRUSH AND A PIECE OF PAPER

DIP YOUR PAINTBRUSH IN THE LEMON JUICE AND WRITE YOUR MESSAGE. PUT MORE LEMON JUICE ON THE PAINT BRUSH AFTER EVERY LETTER.

LEAVE THE MESSAGE TO DRY THEN SEND IT

WHEN YOUR FRIEND WANTS TO READ YOUR MESSAGE THEY JUST PUT IT FACE DOWN IN THE OVEN. (THE OVEN SHOULD BE HEATED TO 175°C OR GAS MARK 4). IT SHOULD TAKE ABOUT 10 MINUTES

THIS WORKS BECAUSE THE HEAT OF THE OVEN BURNS THE LEMON JUICE BUT NOT THE PAPER. BURNING CHANGES THE LEMON JUICE AND MAKES IT GO BROWN

Concentration-camp prisoners would probably not have lemons so they would have to use sweat, saliva or pee as invisible ink. They aren't so healthy – stick to lemon juice.

The postcards with secret messages were meant to be read and destroyed, but some survived. One was put on display in 1997. The card was a simple message:

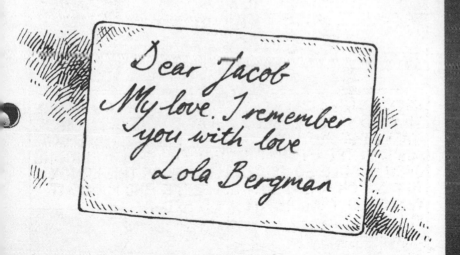

Dear Jacob
My love. I remember
you with love
Lola Bergman

But when the invisible message was read it gave a glimpse of the horrifying truth…

DEATH CAMP. THE REST IS A LIE. HUNGER, STARVATION, DOG FOOD OAT PORRIDGE. AN EPIDEMIC. TORTURE. TORTURE CHAMBER. HUMILIATION. VIOLENCE TERROR. FRIGHT KILLING BY GAS. EXECUTION. GALLOWS. MURDER. INCINERATOR. AGONIZING HELL. OTTO.

It is believed that 'Otto' was Otto Haas, an Austrian who ended up in the death camp because he opposed Hitler.

Ruthless reprisals

Not all Germans were Nazis and not all Nazis were nasty. But there were times in the Second World War when the Nazis behaved as nastily as anyone in the history of the world.

One thing which seemed to bring out their viciousness was revenge. If one Nazi was hurt then a hundred innocent people had to suffer, to set an example to the rest. They were called 'reprisals'. On 22 March 1941 a London magazine carried this awful report…

The London Magazine

Nazi Atrocity in Poland

Following the death of a German soldier, 100 Polish men were rounded up – most of them Jews – and marched through the streets with their hands tied behind their heads. They were ordered to dig their own graves and, to satisfy the barbaric cruelty of the soldiers, forced to perform a 'dance of Death' at the point of a bayonet for the Germans' amusement. There were various methods of execution, some shot, some hanged and others tied to posts and stoned to death.

Nazi violence wasn't only directed at the Jews. In Czechoslovakia in 1942 there was a similar act of cruelty…

Czechoslovakia Today

11 June 1942

Massacre at Lidice

Hitler's henchman, Reinhard Heydrich, was killed by a freedom fighter's bomb in the Czech capital Prague one week ago.

Heydrich - killed

Yesterday the German SS exacted their revenge on the Czech town of Lidice.

They rounded up the inhabitants of Lidice and shot 173 men. Several women were shot while trying to escape and the rest were transported to Ravensbrück concentration camp. The children who could be 'Germanized' were given new names and sent to Germany to be raised by German families.

Today the SS will dynamite the town and the rubble will be levelled so that not a trace remains.

Of the women sent to the concentration camp, 52 died at Ravensbrück – seven of them exterminated by poison gas.

Two years later, in a French village, not even the women and children were spared...

FRENCH UNDERGROUND NEWS

Terror attack at Oradour-sur-Glane

Nazis may call their actions at the little village of Oradour 'revenge'– the rest of the world will call it bloody murder. The German forces massacred everyone they could find in the town and some 642 people were killed.

The Nazis marched into the town demanding to see identity papers and searched for explosives. The recent capture of an SS officer by the French Resistance fighters in the region had infuriated the Germans. Witnesses say the Germans herded the men into the barns and barred the women and children in the church.

Then the killings began. The 190 men were shot first and then smoke was seen rising from the farmhouses as the SS bullies burned them. Finally the church was set on fire; women who tried to escape were machine gunned through the church windows and grenades thrown into the screaming masses killed many more. Two hundred and seven women and children died.

Somehow ten lucky people survived by pretending to be dead till the SS left.

When the war was over a search was made for the Nazis responsible. In 1953, 20 were found guilty of a war crime at Oradour. Five were sent to prison – two were executed. The abandoned village has been left in ruins as a memorial to the victims, with a single English word at the entrance of the village: *Remember*. What made this tragedy even more horrible is that the Nazis had wiped out the *wrong* village. The German officer had been killed in Oradour-sur-Vayres, south of Limoges. The avengers killed the people of Oradour-sur-Glane, to the north of Limoges.

Wild weapons

In wartime the side with the best weapons has an advantage. Potty profs and brainy boffins raced to create new ways of battering buildings, chewing up children, walloping women, splattering soldiers and pulverising pensioners.

The Brits invented Pykrete – a mixture of sawdust and water that was frozen to make a material tougher than concrete. Ships built of Pykrete would be unsinkable and win the war. The war ended before they could be built. Sounds daft – but it's terribly true.

Here are some of the Second World War's brightest brainwaves, all believed to be in existence. Some were just rotten rumours – while others were terribly true. Can you tell which are which?

1 The Molotov cocktail

2 The airblast gun

3 The swimming tank

4 The superfast rocket

5 The submarine aircraft carrier

6 Exploding dogs

Answers

1 The Molotov cocktail. It may seem a stupid idea to attack a tank with a bottle of paraffin … but terribly true! Vyacheslav Mikhaylovich Molotov served in the Soviet war cabinet and they were desperate for weapons to stop the German tanks advancing. Molotov ordered the manufacture of millions of these simple bombs and they are still made by terrorists today – and still called Molotov cocktails.

Some of them worked. It isn't nearly as safe inside a tank as you'd imagine. In north-west Europe mud and ice were the enemies of UK tanks. In mud, it was known for tanks to churn themselves in until only the turret remained visible.

IF I'D WANTED TO BE IN SUBMARINES I'D HAVE JOINED THE NAVY

On ice, Churchill tanks and others which were not equipped with rubber-plated tracks (unlike the US Sherman tanks) became giant uncontrollable toboggans.

To be trapped in a tank on fire was fatal. The hatches were too small for a quick escape. A US officer described a tank fire…

A tank that is hit belches forth long searing tongues of orange flame from every hatch. As ammunition explodes in the interior, the hull is racked by violent convulsions and sparks erupt from the spout of the barrel like the fireballs of a Roman candle. Silver rivulets of molten aluminium pour from the engine like tears.

Germans called Brit soldiers Tommies and they nicknamed their tanks 'Tommy cookers'. US soldiers called them 'Ronson lighters' because of Ronson's advert that said their lighters 'light first time.'

So Molotov cocktails were simple, but deadly – if you could get close enough to a tank to throw it without being shot!

2 The airblast gun. A brilliant idea! Sadly it was just a rotten rumour spread around Germany. But it's such a good idea perhaps you could try it in your own classroom.

ADAM'S GOT AN AIR BLAST GUN DOWN THE BACK OF HIS TROUSERS

PTHRRRP

3 The swimming tank. Another daft idea – but terribly true! On D-Day, British 'DD Tanks' (Dual Drive) were launched from landing craft to 'swim' to the beach. Each tank had a canvas skirt and propeller. They were designed for a short journey over calm, shallow waters. Thirty-two were set off. But the sea was rough and they were launched too far out because naval crews were too scared to go any closer to the beach. Twenty-seven sank like stones, drowning all the crews.

4 The superfast rocket. Another rotten rumour from the Germans – who seemed to believe it. You can see why. A really fast rocket could easily travel as fast as a speeding bullet. But … if the rocket is travelling at (say) 1,000 miles an hour then the bullets in its guns are also travelling at 1,000 miles an hour before they are even fired. Fire those bullets at (say) 500 mph and they're then travelling at 1,500 mph, aren't they? Er … I think that's right. Never mind. The idea of a missile firing bullets is daft enough.

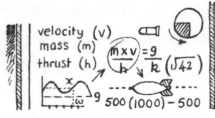

CERONIMO!

5 The submarine aircraft carrier. An absolutely crazy Japanese idea … but it was terribly true. And it worked! The Americans had bombed Tokyo so the Japanese made this plan to get revenge. On 9 September 1942 Japanese submarine I25 surfaced and the pilot, Nobuo Fujita, was sent off to drop fire bombs on the forests of Oregon. The idea was the fires would spread to the west coast US cities and create panic. Only one of his four bombs went off and the small fire was easily put out by the forest rangers. Nice try Nobuo, the only man to drop bombs on mainland USA.

6 Exploding dogs. A sick, sorry and stupid idea, but terribly true, and it worked ... sort of. It was a Soviet idea. The dogs were trained and taken on to the battlefield where the Soviets faced the Germans. Each dog had a mine strapped to its back. They were released and ran straight under the tanks. Unfortunately ... the dogs had been trained using Soviet tanks so, of course, they ran under the Soviet tanks. The tanks were blown apart and the dogs didn't look too healthy either.

Awesome Animals

Animals don't start wars but they certainly suffer in them. Vegetarians and veterinarians may wish to skip this section.

Cruel for creatures?

1 In the First World War the British Army had won with the help of horses – they pulled the guns, carried supplies and made a tasty meal when food was hard to find. But by the Second World War horses had no chance. In September 1939, Polish Cavalry charged the German Panzer tanks. A German soldier said:

In a few minutes the cavalry lay in a smoking, screaming mass of dismembered and disembowelled men and horses.

2 Animals provided sport for bored soldiers. Horse racing was impossible but US soldiers who invaded Italy enjoyed gambling on beetle races instead.

• Each man had his own beetle and painted his 'racing colours' on the insect's back.

• A two-metre circle was drawn on the ground.

• The beetles were placed under a glass jar in the centre of the circle.

• The jar was lifted.

• The first beetle to crawl out of the circle was the winner.

Top-class racing beetles were bought and sold, a lot of money was won and lost gambling on the races.

3 As the war ended, and the Soviet army closed in on Berlin, the German defenders drew back to defend Tiergarten Park. In the park was a zoo. On the morning of 2 May 1945 soldiers began to surrender to the sound of starving and wounded animals. But a Russian remembered the saddest sound was an old zoo keeper – the last one left – weeping over the body of a huge hippopotamus. It had been killed by a Soviet shell.

4 When Dresden was bombed in 1945, 48 circus horses were killed and left by the river Elbe. The same raid had smashed the zoo cages. The vultures escaped and found the dead horses. Six weeks after the bombing people were still reporting seeing escaped monkeys and even a lion.

I'M NOT GOING TO EAT YOU BUT THE AMERICANS MIGHT

5 Adolf Hitler liked dogs. While he was fighting in the First World War he had a little pet dog called Fuschl and he trained it to run up and down ladders. (Somebody pinched the dog and he never saw it again – unless it was served up to him in a pie.) Then Hitler had Alsatian dogs as pets and his wartime pet was called Blondi. When Hitler's friends decided to kill themselves in 1945 old Hitler offered to test the cyanide poison to see if it worked. He fed it to Blondi. It worked quickly and fairly painlessly.

6 Hitler was a vegetarian and hated to see creatures suffer. Lobsters are best cooked by dropping them into boiling water, alive. Hitler hated to hear the screaming sound that they made when dropped into the water and passed a law saying they had to be killed with kinder methods. So it was a good war for lobsters as well as for foxes and deer because Hitler also banned hunting animals with dogs. Of course, it was fine for his Nazis to hunt down and murder humans!

TERRIBLY CRUEL! OUGHT TO BAN IT!

7 Hitler's chief mass murderer, Heinrich Himmler, was keen to have non-Germans put into concentration camps, tortured, experimented upon, gassed, shot, beaten or simply worked to death. Yet Himmler said...

> *Shooting birds and animals is not sport. It is pure murder. We Germans have always had a respect for animals.*

He even considered his SS[3] killers should wear bells at night so any little creatures would hear them coming,

3 The SS (short for Schutzstaffel) were Hitler's personal bodyguard – by the end of the war there were 50,000 of them! Just how much body did the madman have to guard? They wore smart black uniforms and were taught to be ruthless and hard-hearted. This was the organization that executed people in the concentration camps.

run away and not be trodden on by accident. Himmler also said that he liked the medieval German custom of putting rats on trial and giving them a chance to behave themselves, rather than be exterminated. Some Nazi regions banned experiments on live animals – vivisection – while allowing experiments on live human victims in the concentration camps.

8 Soviet prisoners in Germany were always hungry. It was a real treat for them to catch a stray dog and eat it. The dogs were hard to catch … they didn't want to end up as dog meat. The starving Soviets begged their German guards to shoot the dogs for them. The guards didn't mind because they thought the dogs were pests and they made good target practice. When a dog was hit the hungry prisoners went crazy. A guard remembered…

When a dog fell the prisoners would fall on it and tear it apart with their bare hands, before it was quite dead. They'd stuff the heart, liver and lungs into their pockets to be eaten later. Then they'd light a fire and skewer pieces of dog meat on splinters of wood and roast it. There were always fights over the largest pieces.

Tails of the unexpected

The Second World War produced lots of strange animal tales too.

Miaow did she do that?

The miracle mouser of London's St Augustine's Church has amazed her owner, Rector Ross. Yesterday he climbed from the rubble of his church to tell of the white cat's purr-fect prediction.

'Faith has been with us for three years,' he told our reporter. 'She kept her kittens on the top floor of the church house. But three days ago she carried them all down to the basement and tucked them into a corner. Every time I carried them back up she took them down again. Then, last night we had a direct hit. The top floor was demolished. But I found Faith and the kittens safe in the basement corner.'

The People's Dispensary for Sick Animals plans to give heroine Faith their silver medal. Even the Bishop of London admitted, 'It certainly makes us paws for thought!'

9 September 1940

Germans quackers for Freda

A Swiss visitor to London has told of a new secret weapon that the German townsfolk of Friedburg have to warn them of Brave Brit air raids. And it's not a marvellous machine – it's a feathered fowl.

The panicking poultry, a duck called Freda, rushed through the streets quacking loudly. The Friedburgers were so scared they took to their shelters – just in time! Because our brave boys in blue battered them with bombs a few moments later.

'The duck saved hundreds of lives!' the visiting Swiss watchmaker told our paper. 'The frightened Friedburgers are so grateful they plan to erect a statue to Freda.'

Of course, we Brits all know what Freda was quacking as she ran through the streets, don't we? 'The British are coming! Duck!'

30 March 1943

Dog-tired hero

12 November 1940

A British Army company in Egypt has its mascot back. The desert troops called the loveable mongrel dog Sandy (of course) but thought they'd seen the last of the mutt. The truck he travelled in after the battle at El Alamein was captured. The men were taken prisoner but the beastly Boche threw sad Sandy out to die in the heat of the desert days and the freezing nights.

Somehow the big-hearted hound walked 140 miles back to Alexandria. He even found his way through the maze of streets back to the company barracks. PTO

158

'It may look like a mangy mongrel but it's got the guts of a British Bulldog!' the Company Sergeant Major said proudly.

No one could accuse super Sandy of being bone idle!

Coo! What a bird!

Yesterday the best of British pigeons, Mary of Exeter, was awarded the Dickin Medal for outstanding courage.

Mary carried secret service messages from Europe back to Britain and on her first mission arrived back with a slashed breast following an attack by a German hawk. These feathered fiends are specially trained by the Boche to bash our brave birds.

Did Mary give up? Is Adolf Hitler sane? No! Two months later the daring dove was back in action and this time returned with pellets in her body and part of her wing blown off. But the vital message got through. Back home in Exeter her pigeon loft was blasted by bombs but somehow marvellous Mary lived to fly another day.

Her handler, Robert Tregowan, said, 'The last time we found her in a field close to home, wounded all over her body and nearly dead with exhaustion. I think she'd have walked home if she'd had to.' She's one weary warrior who's really earned her corn!

27 February 1945

Mutt medal misery

When the Allied armies landed in Sicily (10 July 1943) an American dog called Chips really earned his dog food by attacking a concrete machine-gun installation. In spite of being wounded, Chips dragged an Italian machine gunner out by the arm and three others surrendered. Soldiers have sometimes captured these strongholds single-handedly, but Chips did it with no hands!

Later the same day he rounded up another ten Italians.

When news of the daring doggy deeds got back to the USA, Chips was awarded a Distinguished Service Cross, a Silver Star medal and a Purple Heart medal – even though it was against army rules to give animals awards.

A commander argued:

> *Brave men shouldn't have to share their awards with a dog.*

So Chips lost his medals. He'd probably have been happier with a bone anyway.

Chilling for Children

Hamburg horror – a grim fairy tale

The little girl limped down the bomb-ruined road, past the hollow houses and stepped carefully round the rubble. She was as thin as the rain that fell and the soles of her shoes were thinner. She clutched a small loaf of black bread to her thin chest.

It was growing dark and she wanted to get home before night fell and the rats came out. Even if they'd been working the twisted lamp posts would not be lit. She stopped. There was a soft, regular click coming from a side alley. She froze and turned her head slowly towards the noise.

A man in a heavy army coat carried a white stick and was groping his way towards her. She stepped back and a stone clattered at her feet. The man stopped, raised his white face and eyes covered by discs of dark glass. He said, 'Is someone there?'

The girl's mouth was dry. She licked her lips and spoke in a small voice. 'Yes, sir.'

The man's worn face gave a small smile. 'A young lady. What's your name?'

'Gerda, sir.'

'Gerda – a lovely name. Gerda, would you like to do something for the Fatherland? Something to help us win this war? Stop the bombs falling each night and set us free?'

Gerda stepped forward. 'Oh, yes, sir!'

'Are you a true German?'

'Yes, sir.'

'Then I can trust you with my secret,' the man said. 'I have a very secret message. It must be delivered now. But I am blind and weak. I need a nimble young person to run like the wind. Do you know Linden Street?'

'Yes, sir.'

'There is a shoe shop at number 27. Go in and tell the old cobbler that Hans sent you,' the soldier said. He reached into the pocket of the great grey overcoat and pulled out a crumpled envelope. 'And give him this. Whatever you do, you must not look in the envelope.'

'No, sir.'

'Good girl. Stop for no one, tell no one, trust no one. Now, run along before it gets dark!'

Gerda took the envelope, turned and ran through the empty streets past the shattered ruin of her old school and the splintered stumps of the trees in the park. The grass was mostly mud and her thin soles slipped as she sprinted across the park lawns. At the far side was the police station, an officer pulling the blackout curtains across watched her.

'Getting dark,' she panted. 'Must deliver the letter and get home before it gets dark.'

Then she stopped so suddenly her feet skidded on the cracked paving. She calmed herself, turned and walked into the police station. The weary old man behind the counter looked at her through red-rimmed eyes. 'Can I help?' he asked and though his thick grey moustache bristled fiercely his voice was kind.

Gerda told her story. The policeman nodded. 'I see,' he nodded. 'Suspicious.'

'That's what I thought!' she cried. 'I suddenly realized as I ran past here! How did he know it was getting dark if he was blind?'

The man picked up a cloak and threw it over his shoulders. 'I think I will take that note to number 27.'

It was later that night, as Gerda lay beneath a

thin blanket and listened to the distant rumble of bombs that there was another rumble. Someone knocking at the door. Her mother showed the policeman into the house and Gerda sat up, wide-eyed, to listen. He told her what had happened.

'There is a cobbler shop at 27 Linden Street, run by an old man and his wife. When I went in the couple looked very nervous. Now all cobbler shops smell of sour old leather but the smell in that shop was worse. The man made an excuse and

went through to the back shop. I heard the back door open then close and realized he'd escaped. So I looked around the shop and then I looked down in the cellar.'

'What was there?' Gerda asked and clutched at her mother's shawl.

'More horrors than I've seen in the whole of this terrible war,' the policeman groaned. 'There were bodies. Dead bodies. Most were cut up and wrapped like joints of meat to be sold to hungry customers.'

Gerda's mother gasped. 'I've heard of people eating human flesh.'

But Gerda had just one question. 'What was in the letter?'

The policeman passed it across to her. She unfolded the paper and read it...

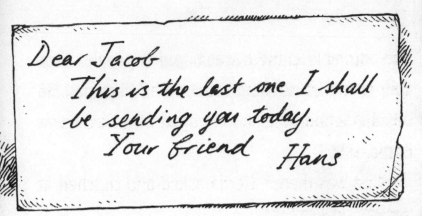

Dear Jacob
    This is the last one I shall
be sending you today.
        Your friend   Hans

Gerda felt faint and giddy. 'I was…'
The policeman nodded. 'You were next.'

Well? A true story? Or just a wartime version of
Red Riding Hood – the girl meeting the stranger
who sends her off to be eaten?

The Second World War was a young people's war. British and US soldiers could be as young as 18. Anyone in the British army aged 30 or over was called 'Dad'!

Teeny terrors

How do you make proper Nazis? Take children and train them. That was the aim of the Hitler Youth movement. But Adolf Hitler and the Nazis didn't invent the idea. At the end of the 1800s Herman Hoffman created the 'Wandervogel' – the German Youth Movement.

Wandervogel Handbook

Rules:

Aims - German youths must discover nature.

Uniform - All members will wear dark shirts and shorts - even in the winter! It will do you good and it will help you discover nature.

Salute - when you meet another member of the movement you must raise your right arm in the air and cry 'Heil'.

In 1936 *all* German boys aged 15 to 18 had to join the Nazi Party Youth Organization – the Jugend (popularly known as the Hitler Youth). You would be called a 'Pimpf' and have to pass a test – sprint 50 metres in 12 seconds, take part in a two-day hike and recite their anthem, 'The Horst Wessel Song.' Wessel was a Nazi thug, killed in a street fight with Communists. The song cheered the Nazis by telling them the ghosts of dead Nazis were marching with them!

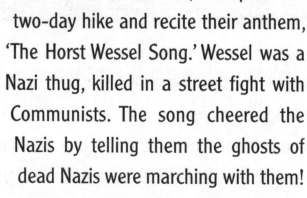

172

Comrades who, though shot by Communists, still march with us, their spirits in our ranks!

Once you'd passed the test you'd be given your Nazi knife with 'Blood and Honour' engraved on the blade. Boys aged ten to 14 could practise being good Nazis by joining a junior Jugend – the Jungvolk – while ten-year-old girls joined the Jungmadel.

Gorgeous girls

The Nazis had a very clear idea of a perfect Nazi woman.

Attention Jungmädel!

Minister Joseph Goebbels has said: 'A woman has the task of being beautiful and bringing children into the world. The hen bird makes herself lovely for her mate and hatches her eggs for him.'

Will you grow to be a beautiful bird?

Remember! Good Nazi girls...

- wear their hair in a bun or plaits
- have blonde hair
- wear no make-up
- wear no lipstick
- do not smoke
- have broad hips
- and never wear trousers!

(You are also reminded that any girl under 18 caught smoking will be sentenced to two months in prison.)

Joseph Goebbels was keen on keeping girls in their place at the kitchen sink. He was Hitler's chief minister by the end of the war. He was weedy and had dark hair and skin so he was a long way from looking like the 'perfect' German he was trying to preserve.

When Hitler died he left the German state to Joseph Goebbels. Goebbels knew he was surrounded by advancing Soviet forces so he poisoned his six children – Helga, Heide, Hilde, Helmut, Holde and Hedda – poisoned his wife, and then himself. But for a few hours the man known as 'The Poisoned

Dwarf'[4] was the Führer of Germany – or at least of the few square yards that were all that was left of Nazi Germany.

4 He was also known as 'God's Mickey Mouse' – which is extremely cruel ... to Mickey!

Evacuees 1

German children were evacuated from bombed cities and sent to camps run by loyal Nazi teachers or old soldiers. Military training was more important than studying. At one camp the children were encouraged to copy from each other rather than fail the exam. You may think that's a good idea and like to see it in your school! But before you suggest it to your head teacher you should be warned – there was a bad side to this camp's rules: if there was a speck of dust found in your room you'd be whipped.

Evacuees 2

British children were evacuated to private houses in the countryside. But the city children were often very rough and their new country homes sometimes very posh.

One grand country lady complained to an evacuee's mother…

The mother grabbed the child, smacked him and reminded him…

Wee war workers

On 30 April 1945, a group of Hitler Youth aged from ten to 14 were taken prisoner in Munich. US soldiers took them to Dachau concentration camp the next day. The boys were forced to help clear away the dead. One of these boys later wrote:

We were taken to a railway siding. We were ordered to open the freight cars… With metal bars we pushed back the doors. The skeleton of a woman fell out. After that nothing more, for the dead bodies were standing so close to one another, like sardines.

They were then taken to work in the crematorium!

Before the war the Hitler Youth movement sounded like bunches of boy scouts and gaggles of girl guides. Would you have wanted to join? And what happened to the young German people who *didn't* want to join?

Rotten for rebels

There's not a lot of information about what happened to rebels who refused to join Hitler's brutal boy scouts. There are some clues, though:

• It seemed that anyone caught enjoying themselves was guilty of wickedness. A shocked Hitler Youth report on a 'swing dance' (a bit like a nightclub today) revealed...

Date: February 1940

Report: Hamburg Swing Festival

The dance music was all English and American.
The dancers made an appalling sight. Sometimes
several couples formed a circle, linking arms
and jumping, slapping hands, even rubbing the
backs of their heads together. And then, bent
double, with the top half of the body hanging
loosely down, long hair flopping in the face,
they dragged themselves round practically on
their knees. Often boys could be seen dancing
together, and each one had two cigarettes in the
mouth, one in each corner...

• The German SS had a section to deal with
'youths' and a special 'youth concentration camp'
was set up to deal with troublemakers. (You can be
sure it would be worse than the worst detention
your school could give you.)

• In 1942 Helmut Hulmut was arrested in Hamburg. What was Helmut Hulmut of Hamburg's crime? He was caught listening to BBC radio programmes! He also handed out anti-Nazi leaflets. His punishment? No, not tortured by being forced to listen to BBC Radio 2 for a week non-stop. But slightly worse. He was executed.

• Jonathan Stark was called to join the army in 1943. He refused to swear an oath to Hitler because Jonathan was a Jehovah's Witness. He was sent to Sachsenhausen camp and in 1944 the young Jon was hanged.

• There were groups of misfits who hung around coffee bars and dressed in clothes the Nazis did not approve of – checked shirts and battered hats –

and even wore rings. These rebels called themselves daring names like the 'Black Gang' or 'Edelweiss Pirates'. (Since edelweiss is a flower this must be a bit like calling your class football team the 'Poppy Pirates'. *That'll* scare the opposition!) Groups like the Edelweiss Pirates sheltered German deserters and escaped prisoners of war, and even attacked the Gestapo. The Chief of the Cologne Gestapo was killed by the Pirates in autumn 1944.

The group members were arrested all over Germany. Lucky members were sent home with their heads shaved, unlucky ones were sent to the special youth concentration camps – and the leaders were hanged in public.

• In 1942 four teenagers put up anti-Nazi posters. You could be fined for this sort of thing today … so don't try this at home! But in 1942 Germany they were simply executed.

• Hans and Sophie Scholl founded the White Rose movement at Munich University to oppose the Nazis. Sophie discovered the ruthless way that Nazis exterminated disabled children while Hans saw brutal actions in the war against Russia. They met up in Munich in 1942 and painted 'Down with Hitler' on university walls. Then they gave out anti-Nazi leaflets – throwing dozens from university windows. They may as well have written, 'We want to be arrested by the SS' on the walls because they had no hope of getting away with it. Both were executed by guillotine.

Fighting small-fry

As the Germans became desperate for soldiers in 1944 there were 16-year-olds fighting on the front line. By the time the Soviets moved into Berlin in 1945 boys of 12 were defending the city.

A 12-year-old German boy found himself in a group of defenders...

I've no rifle. What should I do?

Cheer.

Blitzed Berlin

School rules can be boring. You want to chew gum in class? The school rules won't let you. You don't like rules. But when war comes rules can disappear. People make their own. Bullies take charge. That's when you'd be glad to see some rules!

A young German boy called Claus described what happened when war came close to Berlin in 1945. Some German soldiers fled, were captured by the German army and shot...

A few deserters, dressed only in underclothes, were dangling on a tree quite near our home. On their chests they had placards reading 'We betrayed the Führer'.

The terror of our district was a small one-legged SS officer who stumped through the streets on crutches, a machine-pistol at the ready, followed by his men. Anyone he didn't like the look of he instantly shot.

The gang went down cellars and dragged all the men outside, giving them rifles and ordering them straight to the fighting. Anyone who hesitated was shot.

The front line was only a few streets away. Everything had run out. The only water was in the cellar of a house several streets away. To get bread one had to join a queue of hundreds, grotesquely adorned with steel helmets, outside the baker's shop at 3 a.m. At 5 a.m. the Soviet guns started. The crowded mass outside the shop pressed closely against the walls but no one moved from his place. Soviet low-flying planes machine-gunned people as they stood in their queues ... In every street dead bodies were left lying where they had fallen. Shopkeepers who had been jealously hoarding stocks not knowing how much longer they would be allowed to now began selling them.

A burst of heavy shells tore to pieces hundreds of women who were waiting in the market hall. Dead and wounded were flung on to wheelbarrows and carted away. The surviving women continued to wait. The Soviets drew nearer, they advanced with flame-throwers. Exhausted German soldiers would stumble in and beg for water. I remember one with a pale quivering face who said, 'We shall do it all right. We'll make our way to the north-west.' But his eyes belied his words. What he wanted to say was, 'Hide me. Give me shelter. I've had enough.' I should have liked to help him but neither of us dared speak. Each might have shot the other as a defeatist.

189

The Holocaust

The Nazis were a gang of bullies. And, like any gang of bullies, they needed victims. Adolf Hitler gave them people to hate. He told them to hate those he considered more animal than human. Who were these supposed sub-humans?

Soviets and Jews were top of the list.

The Nazis set about conquering the Soviets, taking control of their lands and using the survivors as slaves.

But the Nazis had a different plan for the Jews. Hitler's henchman, Heydrich, said:

We must exterminate the Jews wherever we find them.

Escape from Hell

On 2 August 1943 the prisoners in Treblinka camp carried out a plan to escape.

• A prisoner made a copy of the key to the gun store.

• The prisoners armed themselves.

• When they were sent to spray the wooden huts with disinfectant they put petrol in the sprayers.

• The huts were set alight.

• As the SS and the Ukranian guards fought the fire the prisoners fought their way out.

• 150 Jews escaped. Although about 100 Jews were recaptured, Treblinka was never rebuilt.

The Nazis tried to destroy the camps when they realized they were losing the war. But the site of Treblinka can still be seen to this day. The memorial stone on the spot says simply, 'Never again.'

Camp humour

One of the ways people survived the concentration camps was to turn the horror around them into humour. A popular Jewish joke in the camps went like this…

The Polish policeman's tale

War was an excuse for some people to act brutally. Today some football matches give hooligans a similar sort of excuse to break the rules, smash property and hurt people. But there are very few football hooligans in a crowd — and there are very few monsters even in a war.

There are more stories of individual courage than of cruelty. How would you have behaved in this situation?

1 The Germans conquered Poland in 1939, of course. But I was one who believed life was better under the Germans than the Soviets who were coming from the west. I had served in Warsaw as a policeman before the war. When the Germans arrived I kept my job and simply said:

2 The Germans gathered the Jews into one area of the city where they could keep their eye on them – the ghetto. My job was to make sure they stayed there. I never liked Jews myself and they never liked me. From time to time we would go into the ghetto, take out the strongest and send them to the labour camps.

3 Even when I heard the stories of Jews being gassed I tried to ignore them. But we all knew that when someone went off to the camps they were never seen again. Soon there were only women and children left in the ghetto. Then one day the German military commander gave us an order.

4 It was true. The houses were like a rats' nest – corridors and stairways and cellars and tunnels where they hid when they knew we were coming. We Polish police knew them best. This raid was to be planned in secrecy. The Jews would have no time to escape. We would seal their secret routes and then drag them out. In the early hours, when they would all be sleeping, we went into the ghetto.

5 But someone had warned them. When we broke down the flimsy doors to their rooms the same sight greeted us.

6 The German Commandant ordered us to search the buildings from cellar to attic. The Commandant himself came along with me. He knew that if anyone could find the Jews it was me. We climbed through the house and I opened every secret panel and trapdoor that I knew about. Every one was empty. At last we reached the top of the house. A ladder led down from a gap in the ceiling.

7 So I took a lantern and began climbing the long ladder. The silence was so great I couldn't believe anyone could be up there in the space below the rafters. But I climbed on. At last I reached the entrance to the loft. If anyone was waiting they could have smashed my head in there and then. I looked over the lip of the hole and shone the lantern in. The light picked out the white faces and wide, dark eyes of 20 women and terrified children. The Commander called up to me.

CAN YOU SEE ANYONE?

8 The reward for taking so many Jews would be great, I knew. I'd be promoted. I'd be a loyal and trusted servant of our conquerors and I would share in their power and wealth. I turned to the Commander and called back down.

Well? What would you have done? You know you'll be sending those women and children to their deaths, but this is war. Thousands are dying every day. What's another 20? And your own wife and family must come first.

What did that Polish policeman do?

Answer

He turned to the German Commander and called, 'There's no one there!' Then he climbed back down the ladder and reported that the house was empty. We don't know what happened to that policeman, but one of the Jewish children survived the war and remembered his curious action that morning. War brings out the worst in some people. It brings out the best in others.

The gentle German

The war wasn't a simple matter of 'good' Allies against 'evil' Nazis. Sometimes the British were known to execute children and many Nazis were known to spare them.

A Jewish mother faced a Lithuanian soldier, working for the Nazis. The Lithuanian raised his gun and pointed it at her head. His finger tightened on the trigger. He was about to kill her for the 'crime' of being Jewish.

Suddenly, a German Army officer stepped forward and rescued her. He turned to the soldier and explained:

One day history will judge us.

History *has* judged the Nazis and generally they have been found 'guilty' – but not all of them.

The woman and her three children survived the war. They lived in a hole under the floor of a barn for almost a year. The hole was about the size of a table. They were four of the 30 survivors in their town. Before the war there had been 25,000.

Epilogue

On 3 September 1939 the *Washington Post* newspaper had a headline that read:

BOTH SIDES AGREE NOT TO BOMB CIVILIANS

Six years later the United States dropped the most horrifying bombs yet invented on the towns of Hiroshima and Nagasaki in Japan.

What changed in those six years? People changed. The world had seen so many horrors that thousands of innocent civilian deaths seemed worthwhile if it meant a quick end to the war.

In 1939, most people really believed that wars were fought only by soldiers. The Second World War changed that for ever. Wars were being fought by everyone; people in the cities as well as men on the battlefields.

An American said, 'Total wars are won by the side with the biggest factories.'

MY FACTORY IS BIGGER THAN YOUR FACTORY!

In the Second World War it had become easier to kill someone when all you had to do was push a button and drop a bomb. You'd never see the suffering you caused. But the real horror of the war was that so many people were prepared to kill so many others in cold blood. A screaming child, a weeping woman or a feeble old man – the killers often showed not one drop of pity. That's what war can do to ordinary people.

They are the things that make the Second World War the most horrible history of all: the innocence of the victims, the vast numbers of them and the unbelievable cruelty of some of the fighters.

That's why truly horrible history can be so important. It helps us to look back at the horror and say the single word from the memorial at the destroyed village of Oradour-sur-Glane:

REMEMBER

WHY IS IT THAT THE ONES WHO MOST NEED TO REMEMBER ARE THE ONES MOST LIKELY TO FORGET?

WOEFUL
SECOND WORLD
WAR

Quiz

Second World War wonders

Try this quick quiz on the Second World War. Replace the words 'Laurel and Hardy'[5] with one of the answers below. One of those answers is 'Laurel and Hardy'!

The missing words in the wrong order are:

UNIFORMS

16-YEAR-OLD BOYS

LAUREL AND HARDY

BONFIRES

NUNS

TOILET ROLLS

WOMEN

PRISON

PARACHUTES

GUILLOTINES

5 If you're not old enough to know who Laurel and Hardy are, then ask your teacher or a parent.

1 British and Allied troops coloured everything khaki brown as camouflage. They even had khaki *Laurel and Hardy*.

2 The British Home Guard were warned that an enemy paratrooper might be disguised as *Laurel and Hardy*.

3 Some spies in Germany were executed by *Laurel and Hardy*.

4 British soldiers in Italy were given summer *Laurel and Hardy* and some died of the cold.

5 In November 1940 a man called Lloyd was arrested in Britain for having *Laurel and Hardy* in his back garden.

6 US paratroopers were safer than British ones because they had two *Laurel and Hardy*.

7 The Germans sent *Laurel and Hardy* into battle when they became short of soldiers.

WELL THIS WAR IS CERTAINLY KEEPING US BUSY OLLIE!

8 The Nazis thought ideal *Laurel and Hardy* should have broad hips.

9 Workers who were late for work in a German factory ended up in *Laurel and Hardy*.

10 Italian leader Mussolini was said to look like one half of *Laurel and Hardy*.

Quick questions

1 When the Second World War started in 1939 civilians were urged to join the Local Defence Volunteers. Comedians said LDV stood for Look, Duck and ... what? (Clue: Vanquish? Not quite.)

2 In May 1940 Mr Hitler did something a certain Mr Fawkes failed to do. What? (Clue: remember?)

3 In 1940 a man was arrested for lighting a cigarette. Why? (Clue: night-light)

4 The British government tried to ban Londoners sheltering in the Underground stations during bombing raids. What did the crafty Cockneys do? (Clue: train for it)

5 Car headlights were masked because of the blackout. How did farmers protect their black cattle that may have strayed on to the road? (Clue: zebra crossing?)

6 Why did parents have to label every piece of their children's clothing during the war? (Clue: bits and pieces)

7 During the war, the tops of pillar-boxes were painted green or yellow. Why?
(Clue: it's a gas)

8 When the war ended in 1945 some children tried to eat bananas without peeling them. Why?
(Clue: Yes! We have no bananas!)

9 In the 1940s you could eat 'chicken fruit on bacon ducks'. What was it?
a) boiled beef and carrots
b) omelette with sun dried tomatoes
c) eggs on fried bread

10 During the Second World War, US soldiers were advised to eat…

a) caterpillars

b) maggots

c) absolutely anything

War-like words?

At the end of the millennium, people were still bombing and killing but they'd found some new words to describe it so that it sounded less horrible. See if you can work out what these military phrases mean.

Words	**Meaning**
1 air support	**a)** human beings
2 friendly fire	**b)** destroy
3 neutralizing	**c)** planes dropping bombs
4 soft targets	**d)** blowing people to pieces by mistake
5 collateral damage	**e)** assassinating a human nuisance
6 immobilize	**f)** shooting soldiers on your own side

Answers

Second World War wonders

1 Toilet rolls. A quick flash of white could give them away to the enemy!

2 Nuns. Or vicars or a woman carrying a baby.

3 Guillotines. In August 1942 German spy catchers uncovered a team of 46 spies. The male spies were hanged, but for some reason the female spies were guillotined.

4 Uniforms. The army planners believed it would be

very hot in Italy, but it was wet and cold and in the mountains it was freezing.

5 Bonfires. Mr Lloyd supported the Nazi party. The magistrate gave Lloyd a prison sentence – Lloyd gave the magistrate a Nazi salute.

6 Parachutes. The British Army said two parachutes took up too much room. The truth was probably that it would have been too expensive.

7 Sixteen-year-old boys. As the war went on and the fit men were killed or captured the German Army called for older men and younger boys to join.

8 Women. The ideal Nazi woman should also have blonde hair, never wear make-up or trousers, and wear her hair in a bun or plaits.

9 Prison. You could be sentenced to three months in prison. (And you thought an hour's detention for being late to school was cruel!)

10 Laurel and Hardy. Mussolini was short and fat. When he became ruler of Italy he wore a dark suit and a bowler hat. Somebody told him he looked just like Oliver Hardy – a comic idiot – so he began dressing in military uniforms instead.

Quick questions answers

1 Vanish. The LDV went on to become the Home Guard, popularly known as 'Dad's Army'.

2 His bombs flattened the Houses of Parliament.

3 He was breaking the blackout laws in force during the war.

4 They bought platform tickets so no one could stop them going down to safety.

5 They painted white stripes down their sides.

6 If the child was blown to pieces then the bits could be identified. Gruesome but true-some.

7 So that droplets of deadly mustard gas would stain the paint and show if there was a gas attack.

8 Many children had never seen a banana and didn't know what to do with it.

9c)

10b) A US Army handbook advised them to eat maggots and grasshoppers (with the wings and legs removed!) but advised against eating caterpillars.

War-like words
1c) 2f) 3e) 4a) 5d) 6b)

Interesting Index

COLLECT THE WHOLE HORRIBLE LOT!

HORRIBLE HISTORIES

SAVAGE STONE AGE

EEK!

WHAT A BOAR!

TERRY DEARY

ILLUSTRATED BY MARTIN BROWN

HORRIBLE HISTORIES®

AWFUL EGYPTIANS

TERRY DEARY

ILLUSTRATED BY
MARTIN BROWN

HORRIBLE HISTORIES

ROTTEN ROMANS

CAESAR WAS 'ERE

MURMILLOS ARE THE BEST

ROMAN LIONS RULE!

TERRY DEARY ILLUSTRATED BY MARTIN BROWN

HORRIBLE HISTORIES

VICIOUS VIKINGS

EEK

ARE WE NEARLY THERE YET?

TERRY DEARY

Illustrated by
Martin Brown

HORRIBLE HISTORIES

OOPS!

Terrifying Tudors

IT'S GOT THE AXE FACTOR!

TERRY DEARY

ILLUSTRATED BY
MARTIN BROWN

WASN'T ME!